Old CARNWATH

Including Braehead, Dolphinton, Dunsyre, Elsrickle, Kaimend, Libberton, Ne

by

Ann Matheson

This view, looking east from the west end of Main Street in the early twentieth century, shows a townscape that has changed little, with the exception of the elevations of the white thatched cottage on the left and the two nearest cottages to the right which have had second stories added. The Walker Memorial Church lies behind the railings on the left.

ACKNOWLEDGEMENTS

Ian and Jennifer Alexander, Alison Coleman, Jack Hoxley, Kathie MacLean,
Jim Ness, Edith Nisbet, Evelyn Stewart, Tam Ward, Biggar Museum Trust.

FURTHER READING

The books listed below were used by the author during her research. None
of them are available from Stenlake Publishing. Those interested in finding
out more are advised to contact their local bookshop or reference library.

Glen, Duncan, *Splendid Lanarkshire*, 1997
Irving, G. V. & Murray, A., *Upper Ward of Lanarkshire*, Vol. 2, 1864
Martin, Daniel, *Upper Clydesdale*, 1999
Nimmo, A. (ed.), *Songs and Ballads of Upper Clydesdale*, 1882
Paul, George, *Another Look at Carnwath*
Smith, Robin, *The Making of Scotland*
Watson, W. J., *History of the Celtic Place Names of Scotland*
Wilson, S. C., *A Contribution to the History of Lanarkshire*
Statistical Account of Scotland, Vol. 10, 1794
New Statistical Account of Scotland, 1834
Third Statistical Account of Scotland, 1960
Scottish census records

This raging torrent is none other than the Medwin Water at Bankhead Farm, photographed on 9 March 1908. Bankhead lies on the valleyside 70 feet above the Medwin's flood plain, about half a mile from its confluence with the River Clyde. Over the centuries, both the Medwin and the Clyde have had many changes of course in this area, cutting across their own meander loops in times of flood. Most Carnwathians will have witnessed scenes similar to this as, despite the building of embankments, flooding remains a problem. Just after the Second World War a gliding club was based at Bankhead, with tractors used to drag the gliders to their take-off point.

INTRODUCTION

The undulating landscape of the Carnwath area is largely the product of the last Ice Age. About 15,000 years ago massive ice sheets began to slide north-eastwards from the Southern Uplands towards the Lothians. These sheets contained stones, sand and gravel that had been scraped and gouged by the ice from the uplands. As the climate grew warmer and the ice began to melt, some of the meltwater flowed through great tunnels under the ice. These rivers carried with them masses of sand and gravel, and when the ice finally disappeared and the rivers dried up, long ridges of deposits were left behind in their tracks. Although commonly known as 'the kames', their correct geological name is 'eskers'. Carnwath's White and Red Lochs are also relics of the Ice Age, formed by lumps of ice which were left stranded in the glacial deposits and later melted to form small lochs or 'kettle lakes'. (A model showing how all this happened can be seen in Moat Park Museum, Biggar.)

After the great ice sheets melted about 10,000 years ago, nomadic hunter-gatherers appeared in the area. Their campsites have been found and dated to between 8,000 and 4,000 BC. Quite recently, evidence of early Stone Age farmers has also been found by Biggar Museum Trust archaeologists, indicating that the Carnwath area was fairly heavily peopled about 6,000 years ago. The moors of the district are rich in archaeological sites dating back c. 5,000 years. These include the large concentration of cairns and burial cairns visible from the Lang Whang. The remains of an Iron Age broch (fortified tower) and a souterrain (underground chamber) at Wester Yardhouses date from about 2,000 years ago. It would be about this time that the name Carnwath, which first appears in written records as 'Karnewid' in 1179, would have originated. Meaning 'cairn in the wood', its origins are Welsh Celtic, and it was named by the Celts who appeared in this part of Britain during the Iron Age. Not long afterwards, in the first century AD, came the Romans, who had a temporary camp near Spittal on the Roman road that ran from Peebles to the west of Scotland, and which would have forded the Medwin just south of Carnwath Mill.

The best-known Carnwath antiquity is the 'pudding bowl' motte on the first fairway of the golf course. This man-made hill would have been the site of the first stronghold of the Somervilles, who were overlords of Carnwath from the twelfth to the seventeenth centuries. Walter Somerville, a Norman baron from Caen, came to Britain with William the Conqueror. In exchange for military and political support, his son William acquired the lands of Carnwath from King David I.

Successive generations of Somervilles made significant contributions to Scottish history. Their names are found on royal charters and Scottish kings visited them at Carnwath to enjoy hunting and hawking on the moors. John Somerville was executed at Newcastle in 1296 for his support of Robert the Bruce. Thomas, who founded the collegiate church at Carnwath c.1425 was one of the ambassadors sent to England to negotiate with Henry V for the ransom and liberation of James I, who was being held by Henry as a political pawn. Thomas's son, William, became a Lord of Parliament in 1445, and in 1451 obtained from James II the charter that made Carnwath a free burgh of barony with the right to have a market cross and hold a weekly market. William's death, however, is a curiosity: it is recorded that he died at Couthally Castle in 1456 'of a surfeit of fruit that came from Cambusnethan'! John, his successor, witnessed James II being killed by the accidental blowing up of a cannon at the siege of Roxburgh in 1460, and later took part in the abduction of the fourteen-year-old James III from Linlithgow to Edinburgh.

In the lead-up to the Reformation of 1560, James Somerville remained loyal to Roman Catholicism and to Mary, Queen of Scots. When she escaped from Lochleven Castle, he raised a troop of 300 men and met her at Hamilton. Severely wounded at the Battle of Langside in 1568, he returned to Couthally Castle where he died a year later. His son, Hugh, became a Protestant and was a member of the jury which found Francis, Earl of Bothwell, guilty of treason in 1592.

The final decades of the Somervilles' tenure in Carnwath were fraught with tragedy. One of Hugh's sons accidentally shot his brother then he himself died about three years later when only 27. Of the remaining sons, Hugh favoured John, the younger, as his successor. This led to costly lawsuits and a siege of Couthally Castle, as Gilbert, the elder son, strove to regain possession. By the beginning of the seventeenth century, the estate was so heavily burdened with debt that it had to be sold. The buyer was John, Earl of Mar, who resold it c.1630 to Robert, Lord Dalyell, who became 1st Earl of Carnwath in 1639. Lord Carnwath was a Royalist, who on several occasions caused offence to the Protestant cause, and consequently had his estates forfeited by the Scottish Convention of Estates. His son received no compensation for his father's losses, and between 1681 and 1685 was forced to sell the barony to Sir George Lockhart, president of the Court of Session. An eminent lawyer, Sir George defended James Mitchell, who was tried in 1678 for attempting to assassinate Archbishop Sharp and the Bishop of Orkney. Having attained several high offices, Lockhart was murdered in 1689 in Edinburgh by Chieslie of Dalry, who was also a landowner in Carnwath. The Lockharts were champions of the exiled Stuarts and Sir George's son, also George (1681–1731), and his brother took part in the 1715 rising. The latter was shot as a rebel at Preston. George's 'Lockhart Papers' are a meticulous account of the history of the Jacobite party. He, along with the town of Carnwath, made strong representations against the Union of the Parliaments in 1707, and his memoirs relating to this were republished in 1995 under the title *Scotland's Ruine*.

While its landlords were involved in affairs of state, Carnwath had its own vigorous life. In medieval times its market would have been the focal point for surrounding villages and hamlets, and locally-grown flax and wool formed the basis of a small domestic weaving industry until the nineteenth century. One of the earliest recorded transactions (1489) notes that John of Carnwath owed John Baty, an Edinburgh burgess, a sack of wool. An Act of Parliament of 1695 granted George Lockhart permission to hold two annual fairs for 'rough sheep'.

In the eighteenth century villagers helped tenant farmers at the harvest and shearing in exchange for the use of a patch of land on which to grow potatoes and a little flax for weaving. The Lowland Clearances of the late eighteenth century saw the end of the old run-rig system and the establishment of large sheep farms, with the result that many cottars saw their livelihoods come to an end and were forced to go to nearby towns for work. Tenant farmers could no longer afford to give up pieces of land for cultivation, so poor villagers also had to leave. Between 1785 and 1793 Carnwath lost 70 people, a trend of depopulation which continued for many years. In 1834 the parish had 181 uninhabited houses.

The *Statistical Account* of 1834 records a population of about 800, mostly weavers producing cloth for the Glasgow market. By 1881, unable to compete with cheaper cloth manufactured by the mills of the Industrial Revolution, only two weavers remained among the town's 300-strong workforce. Following the opening of the station in 1848, employment in Carnwath was still essentially based on agriculture, with a third of the workforce employed as farm labourers, servants, dairy maids etc. Railway employees, of varying status, made up another eleven percent and the rest provided goods and services for the townsfolk and the surrounding catchment area. At this period in its history, and assuredly at many other times, Carnwath appears to have been a vigorous community. *Songs and Ballads of Upper Clydesdale*, compiled by Archie Nimmo of Carnwath, was published in 1882, providing a unique insight into the prevailing culture. It celebrates many aspects of Carnwath life: its fairs; the pleasures of curling on the White Loch; the town's Jacobite escapades; the heroic drunkenness of the Brass Band; the Covenanters; and various locals of notoriety. Two of the most humorous poems recall the 'Carnwath Parliaments' in John Copland's shop and Morris's smiddy, where social and political issues were hotly debated.

By the mid-twentieth century Carnwath had largely become a commuter village, with most of its resident workers employed by the railways and mines, plus the retail trade and other service industries. Kersewell Agricultural School (later college) was established by Lanarkshire County Council in 1954 and the Ministry of Health opened the State Institution at West End in 1948. In 1989, DAR (Data Analysis and Research) of Carnwath was awarded the Scottish Business Enterprise award and in 1992 employed 100 people providing advice to pharmaceutical firms.

At the start of the twenty-first century Carnwath remains a commuter village, but with a considerable amount of local employment. While its roots remain sturdily fixed in its agricultural economy, its rich history may become the foundation of an embryonic tourist industry which is already featured on several websites. Perhaps now is the time to rediscover the 'sulphurous and chalybeate springs' noted near the village in 1799, and to establish Carnwath as a spa town, or even a focal point for recreational activities . . . as enjoyed by Scottish kings!

This row of thatched cottages was demolished at the end of the nineteenth century to make way for the draper's shop of T. S. Clark & Sons. Thomas Somerville Clark was born in Carnwath *c*.1836/7, and when he and his wife Catherine set up in business in the 1860s they sold material manufactured by local handloom weavers. Described as 'drugget manufacturers' in Newbigging in the 1881 census (drugget was a coarse woven fabric used as a floor or table covering), Thomas and his family moved to larger premises next to Carnwath post office in 1891. As the business continued to expand they purchased Pouts Hall Houses (one of which served as Ballantine's shop) and the two-storey building adjoining them.

An Up-to-date Drapery Establishment.

T. S. CLARK & SONS,

Central Stores,

Carnwath.

By 1908 this elegant two-storey building, made of red sandstone from Greenaton Mair, had replaced the old thatched cottages. The family also operated a mail-order business from here, advertised as 'The Mail Order House of the North'. Glenlyon Tweeds were reputed to be 'as sturdy and strong as the men who wear them' and their knickers 'splendid value for the money'! The Clarks generated their own electricity for the shop and houses, and this postcard was printed for the firm's use. On the back it reads 'Our Mr John Clark will call upon you on Friday with a full Range of Patterns and Illustrations of our Newest Goods, when your esteemed orders shall have our careful and prompt attention.'

Two-storey Pouts Hall, next door to the Clarks' shop, acquired a third floor in 1902. Thomas Clark and his wife lived there while their sons George and Jim lived with their own families above the shop. A third son, John, moved away to start an Edinburgh branch of the firm in 1910. Opposite the shop is the junction with the Biggar Road. This part of Carnwath is still known as 'the Toll' because of the presence of the former tollhouse at this location.

This postcard of the Toll was sent in 1925, by which time the Clarks' shop had acquired a third storey. Until *c*.1934 there were no officially named streets or numbered houses in Carnwath. Many buildings had vennels or closes leading to the two 'back rows', the roads running parallel to Main Street, which later became North Road and Murray Terrace. Up to 1879, when tolls were abolished, money for road maintenance came from travellers, who had to pay levies at tollhouses for using particular stretches of road. Toll-keepers bid for the privilege of operating a tollhouse for a year. As the amounts paid for a lucrative stretch of road were often large, toll-keepers frequently sold copious quantities of drink to help pay the rent! The message on this card refers to the post office as being 'at the back of the motor' and describes Carnwath as 'a lovely place, very clean'.

Following the granting of the royal charter (1451) which made Carnwath a free burgh of barony with the right to hold weekly markets, a mercat cross was erected by Hugh, 5th Lord Somerville, in 1516. The urn was blown down during a gale in 1962, repaired and finally replaced in 1970. An inscription on the shaft gives mileages from Edinburgh to Ayr and Peebles to Glasgow. Behind the cross is the tolbooth or 'jail' where justice was dispensed for 400 years until the building's demolition in 1929; this photograph was taken shortly beforehand in May 1928. In the early twentieth century, the ground floor of the tolbooth housed Somerville's cycle and motor accessories shop.

Behind the cross was Morris's smiddy, where the 'Carnwath Parliament' regularly debated the issues of the day:

Your great men of science – Locke, Newton and Bacon
Have often been found to be greatly mistaken;
In truth little better than poor Irish Biddy,
Is a fact often proved in Morris's smiddy.

Carnwath

Any view of Carnwath's east end is dominated by the Wee Bush, the eighteenth century inn which juts out at right angles to Main Street. In 1749 the Revd George Mark complained bitterly about the quantities of alcohol consumed in the village. At that time there were six public houses, as well as five shops which sold 'small beer, porter and whisky'. Revd Mark described the amounts drunk as 'almost incredible' and destined to 'debauch the morals of the lower classes'. The Wee Bush was built to be of service to drouthy travellers, being situated on the Lanark–Peebles turnpike road. The white building on the right was Main the tailor's shop, while the nearest door marked the entrance to the saddler's shop of Willie Paxton, above which was the Masons' hall. Note the two men pumping water from the street pump. Gravitational water came to the village in 1898.

The length of Main Street is seen to good effect in this 1928 photograph, looking west from Townhead to the main part of the village. Just behind the photographer, on the right-hand side of the road, was an area of common land where feu-holders had the right to graze cattle and travelling folk were permitted to camp (for one night only). In their title deeds Main Street householders also have right of access to peat banks. The road known locally as Bareflats led to these peat banks, which were situated north of the village at the intersection of the Peebles–Lanark road with the road to Edinburgh. The latter is known as the 'Lang Whang' (whang is Scots for a bootlace or a long stretch of narrow road). The former tollhouse situated about a mile north of here on the Lang Whang is still occupied.

Take away the water pump, telegraph poles and distant carriages, add some road surfacing, and this could almost be Carnwath today! The third building on the left is the second shop of Main the tailor. Beyond it is an ironmonger's, then a jeweller's shop. In the 1830s Revd James Walker recorded that the streets were much improved, being no longer 'encumbered with dung-hills and peat-stacks', going on to note that 'many of the new houses are handsome'. This postcard view from the early years of the twentieth century suggests there had been no backsliding since then!

Carnwath

Despite its relatively modern appearance today, the house furthest from the camera on the right, fronted by the curving wall, dates back to the eighteenth century when it was the property of James Meikle, surgeon. In 1939 it was completely renovated and new, larger windows installed; at the same time the original lintel stone was reinstated above the door. It reads 'House of the Healer' in Hebrew script. In 1757 James Meikle, whose father George had also been a surgeon in Carnwath, was forced, for financial reasons, to join the Royal Navy as a second surgeon's mate. During the Seven Years War with France he took part in several secret expeditions before returning to Carnwath in 1779, when he married Agnes Smith. Elizabeth, the eldest daughter of his second wife, Helen Hogg, married Andrew Smith, who in 1837 established the bakery that would serve the Carnwath public for 160 years. The woman in the white coat is standing at the door of Smith's bakery. The door in the wall across the street led to the old manse of the United Free (UF) Church. It has been suggested that the Somerville residence, referred to as 'the double tour [i.e. tower] in Carnwath toune', may have been located near here.

The White Loch is a relic of the last Ice Age, a kettle lake produced when an enormous iceberg embedded in glacial debris melted, filling up the hollow the ice had occupied with water. It was once a popular place for curling, but with increases in global temperatures it is unlikely that the loch will be used for another match in the foreseeable future. The anonymous writer of a poem called 'The Ice-Bound Wave', written for Carnwath Curling Club in the nineteenth century, celebrates the pleasures of curling on the loch, while expressing pity for those denied such pleasure:

> The warm climes o the south, where the sun ever shines
> May boast o their myrtles and rich laden vines;
> Though the choicest productions of nature they have,
> Yet they never knew the joys o the ice-bound wave.

Another remarkably modern and sparklingly literate poem about the White Loch was written by James Graeme in 1766. It contains a detailed description of the game and the après-curling:

> The bonspiel o'er, hungry and cold they hie
> To the next alehouse, where the game is played
> Again, and yet again, over the jug.

Sent to a recipient in Glasgow in 1929, this postcard bears the intriguing message: 'Having a great time here. Met your friend Mr Clark and his brothers, rather a jolly fellow but you would like his brothers better if you seen [sic] him'.

This photograph shows Biggar Road in 1897 and was taken at Carnwath's then southern boundary. The two girls are perhaps off for a picnic on the Medwin meanders. On the left is the two-storey building that became the new United Free Church manse when the former manse on Main Street was sold. The building on the right, with the crow-stepped gable, was the police station until the 1960s when it became the doctor's surgery.

This view of William Prentice's boot and shoemaker's shop bears the enigmatic message: 'Very sorry, but it canna be. Will write later on.' It was sent to Mrs Moffat of Braehead, Saltcoats by 'MP'.

This postcard was published by Mr J. Jackson, stationer of Carluke, who took the photograph from which it was produced in October 1902. Before the ferry across the Clyde at Lampits was established in 1829, it was impossible to ford the river here for nine months of the year. Consequently, the route to Pettinain was nine miles long rather than the two and a half miles as the crow flies. The ferry, described as a float, was attached to a chain stretched between the two banks of the river which it used to pull itself across. In this view Andrew Cullen is winding the chain to transport Smith the baker's van across the water. The van is accompanied by Jimmy Grossart. During the 1920s the government made Lampits Farm (background) a centre for unemployed youths, who were given an agricultural training to prepare them for emigration to Canada. The scheme ended in the 1930s when employment prospects in Lanarkshire's heavy industries improved.

Carnwath station opened in 1848 on the Edinburgh branch of the Caledonian Railway's line from Carstairs Junction. This photograph, showing the station and Jackson's slaughterhouse (left), was taken *c*.1908. The flat area on the left is now the site of the council's salt depot. Nothing of the station remains.

This sheltered footpath, which was often covered in pine needles, provided a very picturesque shortcut to the station, situated about half a mile west of the village. Up to the mid-1960s schoolchildren who attended Lanark Grammar School walked daily along this path, which was haphazardly lit by intermittent paraffin lamps. The path was also one leg of a popular circular walk, linking with the old coach road and back to the A721. Most of the trees have now been felled.

The railway bridge at Lampits carried the old Dolphinton line, which ran east from Carstairs Junction to link with the Peebles to Edinburgh line at Leadburn. The line closed to passengers in 1945 and to freight in 1950. One of America's richest men, Paul Mitchell (of Mitchell Hair Systems), was born in the cottages beyond the bridge. His father, who later became inspector for the royal residences in London, was electrician at the Lampits government training centre just after the First World War. His mother, Jenny (née Foster) lived near the Wee Bush in Main Street, Carnwath. Today only the pillars of the bridge remain.

Carnwath from Golf Course.

Carnwath golf course was founded as a 9-hole course (as seen here) on the south side of the main road from Lanark in 1907. During the 1920s it expanded north of the A721. Although less than 6,000 yards long, the course is a challenging one as it is sited on undulating glacial deposits and several roads and a railway line have to be negotiated!

The 'Disastrous Band' leads Carnwath's fancy dress parade on 8 July 1905. Another apparently disastrous band was celebrated in an anonymous poem published in *Songs and Ballads of Upper Clydesdale* in 1882:

> Their music loud and strong re-echoed to the skies,
> The very hares and foxes were filled wi surprise;
> Some little hills micht dance, but auld Tintoc made a stand,
> Astonished at the strains o Carnwath Brass Band.
>
> But oh, the last St John's Day they got an unco fa;
> Altho it was winter, it was neither frost nor snaw;
> Yet they drank themselves so drunk that some could scarcely stand!
> And wasna that a shame to Carnwath Brass Band?

A large crowd has gathered to watch the start of the 1909 Red Hose Race, the winner of which was W. Hunter from Shotts. Claimed to be the oldest foot-race in Scotland, the tradition dates back to 1507. Symbolic of an intriguing legal arrangement between the Barony of Carnwath and the Scottish Crown, it was negotiated by Sir John Somerville of Quothquan while he was acting as guardian to his nephew Lord John Somerville. A royal charter was drawn up by King James IV which, in effect, made Carnwath independent of the Crown in return for a nominal payment. In this case, the whimsical payment agreed was: 'two pairs of red hose, made of two half-ells of English cloth, to be awarded on the Feast of St John, at the midsummer, to the person who could run fastest from the East end to the Hale Cross'. Despite this agreeable arrangement arrived at through Sir John of Quothquan's amicable relationship with the king, it later became apparent that Sir John did not have his nephew's best interests at heart, as he managed to acquire considerable lands and revenues from the estate during the period of his guardianship.

Carnwath House (seen here in 1928) was demolished in 1970 to make way for a new clubhouse for the golf course. Although mainly dating from the early nineteenth century, it retained traces of a sixteenth/seventeenth century fortified house which would have been a residence of the Somervilles. The Lockharts, who purchased the Barony of Carnwath in the 1680s, only used the house as a hunting seat. The family were staunch Jacobites, and Archie Nimmo, editor of *Songs and Ballads of Upper Clydesdale*, described the arrival of Jacobite rebels in Carnwath one Sunday when local people were in church. Thoroughly alarmed, the minister prayed for divine protection, asking the Lord to 'put hooks in their noses and bridles in their jaws and turn them back the way they came'. The rebels apparently took possession of Carnwath House and seized a number of horses, which were later restored to their owners by George Lockhart's son, who was at Broughton with the rebel army. According to Archie Nimmo's story, young George visited Carnwath House after Culloden, mounted on Bonnie Prince Charlie's horse, resulting in a local mob arriving to apprehend him. However, he vanished and finally escaped to France on the same ship as Prince Charles himself.

Carnwath Recreation Park.

The tennis courts, bowling green, play park and art deco style pavilion were all built in 1936 to celebrate the accession of King George VI that year and his coronation in 1937. Alison and John Coleman were the main founders of Carnwath Tennis Club in 1949.

TINTO FROM THE PLAYPARK, CARNWATH. 1332.

This nostalgic view showing the play park in the 1950s looks south to Tinto Hill (707m), the dominant peak in this part of Lanarkshire. Beyond and to the right of the hedge was the 'Blin Well', once one of the village's main sources of water. Women from the west end of Carnwath used to wash and bleach their clothes here.

Three local men examine the remains of a Spitfire aircraft which crashed on the golf course on 12 March 1944. Eyewitness accounts suggested that the pilot made heroic efforts to avoid hitting the village. The plane, which had been searching for a Liberator bomber that was lost in poor visibility, was returning to its base. The pilot, Flight Sergeant Charles Sayer, was killed.

24

Flags are flying and everyone is dressed in his or her Sunday best to celebrate Pretoria Day on 6 June 1900. After a series of British defeats in the Boer War (1899–1902), the occupation of Pretoria by the British on 31 May 1900 marked the culmination of a run of victories against the Boers. Guerrilla warfare continued until 31 May 1902, when the Boers finally agreed to accept British sovereignty.

The nineteenth century saw Carnwath's economy alter radically. At the start of the century most of the village's workers were handloom weavers, producing cloth for local sale or the Glasgow market. However, domestic weaving declined rapidly as handloom weavers were undercut by cheaper cloth manufactured in the mills of the Industrial Revolution. By the 1881 census only two families of weavers remained: Hugh Kelly and his wife, Christina; and William Kelly and his wife, Sarah. This photograph of one of the Kelly couples was taken in the 1890s.

Nineteenth century census records refer to this row of weavers' cottages as 'Back Row South Side'. Now called Murray Terrace, some of the cottages are still in use, mainly for storage or as lockups adjoining Main Street properties.

Cows and sheep progress down Main Street past Mains' drapery. In the nineteenth century, cows were summoned to the common grazing land at Townhead by the village drummer boy. This early twentieth century photograph was probably taken when cattle were being driven back to the village after a show day. The agricultural show continues to be one of Carnwath's most important annual events. A local worthy, Willie Woodcock, used to attend the shows offering to 'Say a prayer for a penny, Mrs'. When he found a willing customer, his response was invariably, 'God bless that bonnie wumman up there. Gie me it noo!'

This photograph of the Carnwath milk cart in Main Street can be accurately dated to 18 July 1897. Surplus milk from the large number of dairy farms in the area was sent to milk distribution centres in Edinburgh, or made locally into Dunlop cheese.

28

Carnwath's parish school dates back to 1615. In the 1830s the Revd James Walker noted of his parishioners that: 'The people are in general anxious to obtain education for their children and the heritors [landowners] laudably pay for the families of paupers'. He added rather optimistically that 'perhaps there are no persons in the parish who are unable to read'. Carnwath Public School (above) was built in 1814, the school itself on the ground floor and the schoolmaster's flat above. Around the wall of the assembly hall were the words: 'Pass through this gateway and seek the light of truth, the way of honour, the will to work for men'. This building became the schoolmaster's house when the new school, built at the Edinburgh road end in 1876, was reconstructed and enlarged in 1913.

Old market towns usually had several inns to provide refreshment for drouthy customers on market days. The Market Inn, well-placed right beside the market cross, was owned by the Somerville family. At the 1881 census, Martha Kay, a widow, was the hotel-keeper. She lived here with her unmarried son and daughter, her grandson, John Kay, and her elder sister, Mary Somerville, who was 64. The photograph is dated 15 September 1898. Note the sign on the wall offering stabling.

Jutting out into Main Street, the eighteenth century New Bush Inn (commonly known as the 'Wee Bush') is one of Carnwath's principal landmarks, well situated to attract erstwhile market day customers and travellers on the Lanark to Peebles turnpike road. Robert Burns visited the inn in 1786, en route to Edinburgh to publish the second edition of his poems. He had spent the previous night at Covington Mains, the house of Archibald Prentice. The inn probably acquired its present name from the motto on Burns's unofficial coat of arms, 'Better a wee bush than nae bield', which appears on the sign on the gable end. This coat of arms became 'official' only in 1988 when, with minor alterations, it was adopted by the Burns Federation. The Walkinshaws (named above the entrance) owned the Wee Bush for some years, and Robert Walkinshaw and his son Jimmy were both world champion quoiters.

The building that became Carnwath Mill was originally an early seventeenth century bastle house, a fortified farmhouse built to protect cattle and their owners from Border raids. The ground floor walls of the bastle, which now form part of the farmhouse, are over a metre thick. In 1635, Wm. Watson of Carnwath Mill made his testament, a will and inventory of all he owned. His worldly goods consisted of an old cow and its heifer (worth between them 20 merks, or just over £13), a stirk, and the contents of his house with his clothing, totalling £20 altogether. However, he was owed about £73, enabling him to leave his family some security. Mr Williamson, the Carnwath schoolmaster, witnessed his testament. Carnwath Mill derives most of its fame from the song, 'We're no awa tae bide awa:

As I cam doon frae Wilsontoon,
I met wee Johnnie Scobie,
Says he tae me, 'Cud ye go a hauf?'
Says I, 'Man, that's ma hobby!'
Sae we had a hauf an anither hauf
An then we had anither,
Till we got fu
An shouted 'Oo!'
'The Carnwath Mill forever!'

FIRE AT KERSWELL APRIL 20TH 1911.

In the early fourteenth century Robert the Bruce granted a charter of the 'lands of Creswell' to Andrew, second son of Sir Archibald de Douglas, Lord of Bothwell. The Chieslie family owned Kersewell for much of the seventeenth century, and in 1689 Sir John Chieslie of Dalry (Edinburgh) murdered Sir George Lockhart, the main landowner of Carnwath Barony. Sir George, an eminent lawyer, had pronounced against Sir John in his divorce proceedings, and the irate Chieslie shot him in the back on his way home from church. Caught red-handed, he was arrested and tortured, his right hand cut off and fixed on the West Port of Edinburgh while his body hung in chains. It is said that his corpse then mysteriously disappeared, to be found 200 years later under the floor of his Edinburgh residence, Dalry House. In the early eighteenth century Kersewell was purchased by Bertram of Nisbet, whose family remained there for 200 years. Wm. Bertram of Kersewell was apparently the only major landowner who actually lived in the parish during the eighteenth century. This fire, on 20 April 1911, severely damaged the building, which was later restored. The sender of another postcard, dated 13 May 1911 and addressed to Lady Ochterlony in Forfarshire, described the building as 'a melancholy ruin'. In 1954 Lanarkshire County Council bought the Kersewell estate for use as an agricultural school for boys aged between twelve and fifteen.

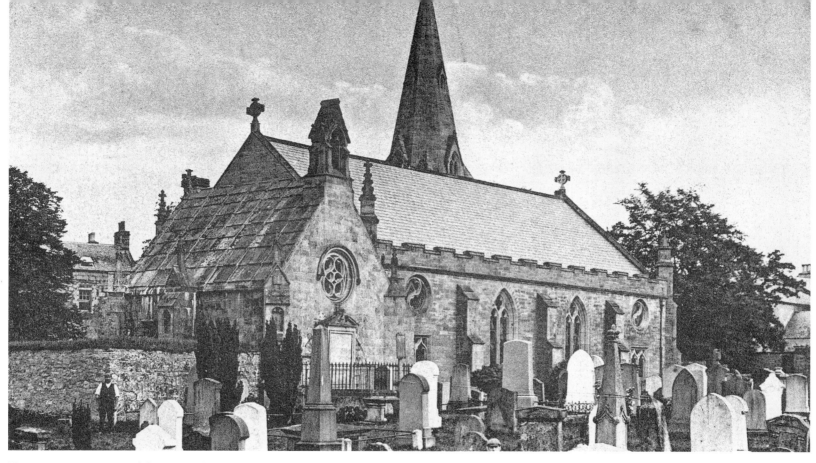

No trace now remains of the original church which stood on this site. This was founded by the Somervilles and owned by them until the middle of the twelfth century, when William de Somerville granted it to the church of Glasgow and its revenues went to support Glasgow Cathedral. Around 1425, Thomas, 1st Lord Somerville, set up a collegiate church (one that had two or more pastors) for a provost and six prebendaries or clergymen. St Mary's Aisle, which stood on the north side of this church, remains as a gem of Gothic architecture. Inside, a mid-sixteenth century altar tomb bears the effigies of Hugh, Lord Somerville, and his wife Janet. Several members of the Somerville and Lockhart families have been buried here. The present church was built in 1867 and is now home to the combined congregations of the United Presbyterian, Free and Established Churches. In the *Concise Scots Dictionary*, 'Carnwath-like' is said to mean 'awkward or odd-looking'. This is no insult to the Carnwath people, but refers to the old church bell which was situated at the eastern end of the church rather than the western end, which was the norm for Scottish churches. This was so unusual that the phrase 'Carnwath-like' came to mean anything that was awkward-looking.

Walter Somerville, a Norman baron from Caen, came to Britain with William the Conqueror. In exchange for the promise of political and military support, King David I (1124–1153) granted Walter's son, William, the lands of Carnwath. The motte pictured here was a man-made hill built for defence, which would have been the site of the first Somerville castle. The Somerville lordship of Carnwath lasted until the early sixteenth century.

The Moat, Carnwath. This is a sand hill of this peculiar shape & is a puzzle to Geologists. R.W.

RUINS OF COWTHALLY CASTLE NEAR CARNWATH

Little remains of Couthally Castle, built by the Somervilles in the mid-twelfth century for defensive purposes. It was built on a narrow, dry site in the middle of boggy land, and had three concentric ditches surrounding it. Despite these measures, the original castle was all but destroyed during the fourteenth century Wars of Independence and had to be rebuilt c.1375. During the interim period, the Somervilles built what was known as 'the double tower' in Carnwath, probably close to where the manse of the UF Church was later erected. By the sixteenth century, Couthally consisted of three separate towers, two square and one round. Hugh, 6th Lord Somerville, joined the towers, adding a hall and various other rooms. King James IV frequently visited Couthally for hawking on the moors, and a number of his charters were signed and dated there.

In 1794 the Revd George Mark wrote: 'On the north side of the Dippool, coal, iron and limestone abound everywhere; the springs and small streams on this side are, in general, hard water, not good for tea, washing or watering flax'. The eighteenth century Roy map shows an ironstone mine just north of Braehead and various limeworks to the south. These raw materials would have gone to feed the Wilsontown Ironworks, which closed in 1842. Despite Braehead's proximity to raw materials for industry, it was described in the 1830s as a small weaving settlement of about 120 people. By 1881 nine weavers remained in the village, and over a third of the workforce were either miners or labourers, presumably in the Forth pits a few miles away. There is certainly no hint of the Industrial Revolution in this postcard view of Main Street sent in 1913.

A group of children enjoy the happiest days of their life (allegedly!) outside Braehead School in the 1910s.

This postcard was sent on 28 August 1908 when Dolphinton could boast two stations! The Caledonian station, pictured above, was the terminus of the Carstairs–Bankhead–Dunsyre–Dolphinton line, which opened in 1867. Although there had been coal pits at Dolphinton, these had been worked out by the time the branch line opened, and its main business was the collection of milk for the Edinburgh market. Lack of traffic brought about its closure to passengers in 1945 and to freight in November 1950.

This was the terminus of the Leadburn, Linton & Dolphinton Railway, which opened in 1862. Taken three years after its closure in 1933, the desolation of the scene speaks for itself.

Dolphinton is first mentioned in records dating from 1253: 'Dolfinston' was the land belonging to Dolfyn, who was a brother of Cospatric, Earl of Dunbar. Nearby Garvald derives its name from the Gaelic *garbh allt*, meaning 'rough stream'. A first-century Roman road ran from Dolphinton to Inveresk. This later became part of the old coach road which preceded the building of the A702 in 1834. Lying on this important route linking the Borders with Edinburgh, Dolphinton must have had many uneasy moments. Revd John Aiton wrote in 1834 that: 'Exposed to the havock (*sic*) of Border raids and Annandale lifters, and thus identified with the most memorable revolutions of the nation, it is probable that in early times but a small proportion of our parishioners died in their beds.'

Dunsyre station was on the Carstairs to Dolphinton line, and it is apparent from this picture that the stationmaster took a great deal of pride in his work. Note the sign advertising the 'Princes St. Station Hotel, Edinburgh', owned by the Caledonian Railway. Before the arrival of the railway, carriers transported local butter, eggs and fowls from the Dunsyre area to Edinburgh three or four times a week.

Dunsyre is a hillfoot settlement on the lower south-facing slopes of Dunsyre Hill (401m), above the marshy flood plain of the South Medwin. The Dunsyre area is rich in archaeological remains dating back to the Stone Age. Although its exact location is unknown, Dunsyre Castle was sited *c*.300–400m south of this view. It was a typical peel tower with a vaulted lower storey and two upper storeys, reached by a circular staircase built into the thickness of the wall. The Dunsyre area played an important role in Covenanting times and there are several 'preaching holes' on the surrounding moorland where preachers hid when the dragoons approached. Donald Cargill preached his last sermon on Dunsyre Common before he was captured at Covington Mill in 1681, taken to Edinburgh and hanged.

Elsrickle looking East.

Though the road is now considerably wider, the house on the right is still recognisable from this early twentieth century postcard. Elsrickle is a ribbon settlement (about half a mile long) on very undulating land lying along the A721. Earliest records show that the lands of Walston and Elgereth (now Elsrickle) belonged to the Lords of Bothwell from the twelfth century. When the infamous 4th Earl of Bothwell lost all his rights, following his alleged role in the murder of Darnley and his subsequent marriage to the ill-fated Mary, Queen of Scots, the barony of Walston was restored to the crown. James VI later granted it to the Earl of Mar.

Elsrickle looking West.

In 1840 Revd James Wilson described Elsrickle as 'a picturesque village' with the potential to become 'the prettiest . . . in the upper ward'. He also reported that 'some good slated houses have lately been erected'. This view of Elsrickle looking west would certainly confirm his opinion.

Kaimend, named for its geographical location at the eastern end of a kame or esker, is situated a mile east of Carnwath on the A721. It was formerly an agricultural village with a small domestic weaving industry. At the 1881 census there were twelve houses (two of them unoccupied), one of which was the tollhouse. Although there has been extensive housing development northwards towards Kersewell, the old nucleus of the village has changed little.

Libberton (Lanarkshire)

Libberton lies two miles south of Carnwath on the B7016, on gently sloping land on the west-facing valley-side of the River Clyde. Sent in 1921, this postcard is a nostalgic reminder of the days before corn stooks were replaced by black polythene rolls. Libberton has always been an agricultural village. Its church was built in 1812 and, according to the poet Blind Harry, Sir Thomas Gray, Parson of Libberton, was one of the companions of William Wallace.

Newbigging's original market cross was erected in the thirteenth century by Walter of Newbigging. The cross shown here is medieval in its eight-point design, and cross and stone are all one piece. The date 1693 and the initials GL (George Lockhart) are cut into the back of the cross. The original had a double cross engraved on it.

Newbigging, Carnwath.

The lands of Newbigging passed to the Somerville family *c.*1250 when William de Somerville married the daughter and heiress of Walter of Newbigging. William de Somerville's grandson later returned the lands to the Newbiggings. In the early nineteenth century, Newbigging had a population of 200, mostly engaged in handloom weaving.

Walston Church stands on an ancient site and is mentioned in many charters dating from the thirteenth century. In one of these (1292) the landowner of Walston, William of Moray, Lord of Bothwell, granted (for the good of his own and his ancestors' souls!) the revenues of Walston Church to Glasgow Cathedral, while retaining the right to choose the church's vicar. The churchyard has some splendid early eighteenth century tombstones, with carved symbols and effigies including one of a blacksmith and one of Robert Wyld who died in 1705. The church became redundant in 1953, when its congregation merged with those of Dunsyre and Dolphinton. Its seventeenth century communion cups are on display in Biggar Moat Park Museum and the church itself is owned by Biggar Museum Trust. Most of the building as seen here dates from large-scale alterations (completed in 1789) to the existing mid-seventeenth century church.